BETWEEN SILENCES

Phoenix · Poets

A SERIES EDITED BY ROBERT VON HALLBERG

HA JIN

BETWEEN SILENCES

A

VOICE

FROM

CHINA

THE UNIVERSITY OF CHICAGO PRESS

Chicago and London

Ha Jin was born in Liaoning, China, in 1956. A former soldier in the People's Army, he is currently a Ph.D. candidate in the Department of English and American Literature at Brandeis University. All of the poems in Between Silences, *Ha Jin's first book, were written in English.*

The University of Chicago Press, Chicago 60637
The University of Chicago Press, Ltd., London
© 1990 by The University of Chicago
All rights reserved. Published 1990
Printed in the United States of America

99 98 97 96 95 94 93 92 91 90   5 4 3 2 1

Library of Congress Cataloging-in-Publication Data
Jin, Ha, 1956–
   Between silences : a voice from China / Ha Jin.
      p.   cm. — (Phoenix poets)
   ISBN 0-226-39986-9 (cloth). — ISBN 0-226-39987-7 (pbk.)
   1. China—Poetry.   I. Title.   II. Series.
PS3560.I6B48   1990
811'.54—dc20   90-10877
                                                                    CIP

⊗ *The paper used in this publication meets the minimum requirements of the American National Standard for Information Sciences—Permanence of Paper for Printed Library Materials, ANSI Z39.48-1984.*

Contents

Preface

*Silence, and silence—either you erupt in
silence, or you perish in silence.*
—Lu Xun

"**H**a Jin" is my pen-name; my true name is Xuefei Jin.

The poems contained in this book mainly present some experience of the 60s and the 70s in China. The experience is not strictly personal, although in most cases I was stimulated by my memory of those hard facts which cannot be worn away by time. There were many things more terrible in the Cultural Revolution. I do not mean to tell horrible stories in this book, and instead I want to present people's feelings about and attitudes towards these events. The people in this book are not merely victims of history. They are also the makers of the history. Without them the history of contemporary China would remain a blank page.

I went to the Chinese Army in December 1969 when I was not yet fourteen, because at that time schools were closed, though we sometimes did go to school copying the quotations of Chairman Mao. It was said that the Russians planned to invade China, so I wanted to defend my country. I preferred to die in a battlefield rather than to be killed at home in an air-raid shelter as a civilian. I served in the army for five years. After that I worked for the Harbin Railroad Company as a telegrapher for three years. In 1978, my school life started again. I got my B.A. degree and my M.A. degree in China. Now I am a graduate student at Brandeis University.

Among my generation I am one of the most fortunate. Unlike millions of people of my age who went to the countryside to be "re-educated," I went to the army, which was a privilege that I could have only because my father was an officer then—although I was also ready to die like other soldiers at the border area between Russia and China. Unlike millions of people of my age who do not have the opportunity to study in formal schools and have to struggle with books at night schools or in adult-education programs, I managed to have some education and am studying abroad.

As a fortunate one I speak for those unfortunate people who suffered, endured or perished at the bottom of life and who created the history and at the same time were fooled or ruined by it. If what has been said in this book is embarrassing, then truth itself is cold and brutal. If not every one of these people, who were never perfect, is worthy of our love, at least their fate deserves our attention and our memory. They should talk and should be talked about.

August 1988

Acknowledgments

Grateful acknowledgment is made to the following magazines in which many of these poems first appeared:

Agni: "A Page from a Schoolboy's Diary," "A Thirteen-Year-Old Accuses His Teacher," "On the 20th National Anniversary," "Promise," "Marching towards Martyrdom," "A Battalion Commander Complains to His Secretary," "A Young Worker's Lament to His Former Girlfriend," "A Brother's Advice," "My Knowledge of the Russian Language."

The Boston Review: "A Hero's Mother Blames Her Daughter," "The Haircut," "A Sacred Mango," "An Older Scholar's Advice."

Brandeis Review: "My Kingdom," "Our Date on the Bridge," "An Editor Meets His Former Girlfriend in a Fish House," "Because We Dare Not Be Ambitious," "A Forced March."

The Paris Review: "The Dead Soldier's Talk."

The Dead Soldier's Talk

*In September 1969, in a shipwreck accident
on the Tuman River, a young Chinese soldier
was drowned saving a plaster statue of
Chairman Mao. He was awarded Merit
Citation 2, and was buried at a mountain
foot in Hunchun County, Jilin.*

I'm tired of lying here.
The mountain and the river are not bad.
Sometimes a bear, a boar, or a deer
                              comes to this place
as if we are a group of outcast comrades.
I feel lonely and I miss home.
It is very cold when winter comes.

I saw you coming just now
like a little cloud wandering over grassland.
I knew it must have been you,
for no other had come for six years.

Why have you brought me wine and meat
                              and paper-money again?
I have told you year after year
that I am not superstitious.
Have you the red treasure book with you?

I have forgotten some quotations.
You know I don't have a good memory.
Again, you left it home.

How about the statue I saved?
Is it still in the museum?
Is our Great Leader in good health?
I wish He live ten thousand years!

Last week I dreamed of our mother
showing my medal to a visitor.
She was still proud of her son
and kept her head up
while going to the fields.
She looked older than last year
and her grey hair troubled my eyes.
I did not see our little sister.
She must be a big girl now.
Has she got a boy friend?

Why are you crying?
Say something to me.
Do you think I can't hear you?
In the early years
you came and stood before my tomb
swearing to follow me as a model.
In recent years
you poured tears every time.

Damn you, why don't you open your mouth?
Something must have happened.
What? Why don't you tell me!

1986.

one

*Towards a
Battlefield*

Again, These Days I Have Been Thinking of You

1

When we were leaving home for the army
you burst into tears on the train.
You said, "I will miss my parents.
I have never travelled that far."
But you also claimed
it was everyone's duty to defend the country,
and you would fight the Russian Revisionists
                    to the dead end.

I lowered my head and did not cry.
But my mother's eyes, dimmed with tears,
were striving in the cold wind
to hold back the train going to the North.

2

On the Northern land
our foot-prints
disappeared in the snow.
The hard ice was slowly
losing its layers.

We didn't have to wear fur hats
on our patrols along the borderline,
and watered our horses at little springs.

3

At last the rain loosened the black earth.
Azaleas bloomed on the mountain slopes.

The woods did not understand war.
The mountains and the rivers did not understand war.

But every night we slept
with our clothes on.

We were prepared to fight.

4

The tanks, which played the enemy,
were running through the valley.
Wooden grenades and rubber bazooka-projectiles
started raining towards them.

Everything was false,
but we did it seriously.

Why did you choose that tank
with a revolving barrel like a gigantic scythe,
to lay an explosive package at its back?

It laid you on the ground
and its caterpillar ran over your limbs.

We carried you down the hill.
Your blood dropped into a small brook
                    flowing towards the Amur.

                    5
White ceilings,
white walls,
white nurses.
Only your black eyes were sliding slowly.

Our eyes collided.
You were staring at me
in deadly silence.

Can you speak?
Can you hear what others say?
You are two feet shorter than before.

You sluggishly turned into your ward
like a startled turtle.

Watching your warped back
I was sending off an epoch.

                    6
Are you still alive?

You are a little dog, abandoned,
often groaning at the door
of my conscience.

Tonight, in the long silence
again I am thinking of you.

The Chinese Communist Party accused the Russian Communist Party of having revised Marxist theory, and therefore the Russians were called "Russian Revisionists" by the Chinese in the late 60s.

The Amur is a long river which forms for more than one thousand miles the border between China and the Soviet Union. Military conflicts broke out on this river in the late 60s.

On the 20th National Anniversary

On the morning of the 20th National Day
my uncle came home and told us:
"All our troops have got into position,
for the Russians may throw an atom-bomb on us today."

After breakfast he returned to the headquarters,
but I had to go to school and join the celebration.

The fear oppressed my back like a bag of sand.
I could not raise the little triangle flag in my hand,
nor could I shout slogans with my classmates.

During the break I called together my best friends
and told them what would occur on this day.
Benli said, "I must go home
and tell my dad to kill all our chickens."
Qingping said, "I must tell my aunt
not to buy a sewing machine.
Who would care about clothes if that happens."
Yimin and I said nothing,
but we knew what we were going to do.

We decided to go to the army,
for we did not want to be roasted at home
like little pigs.

Promise

On the evening before I left for the army
you made dumplings with shrimps and leek.
You put in all the kinds of spices we had
and for the first time you allowed me
to touch white spirit. My little brothers and sisters
said they never had dumplings so delicious
and all ate to their hearts' content.
But that evening you didn't eat.

After they had gone to bed,
you and I sat face to face.
You broke the silence with your quiet voice:
"Your father is with his troops in the mountains
and can't see you off, but I know
what he would say if he were here.
You are going to the border area
and anything may happen to you.
If you are caught by the enemy,
you must never give up, and never
betray our country and our people.
Please promise me."

Your demand was so weak
that I did not have to promise you.
"Go to bed, Mom. Please don't
think of such a bad thing.
I will be all right."
All at once I became a big man,
and you obeyed me.
But before you went away
you murmured, as if to yourself,
"I hope they put you in a headquarters.
You are too young, just fourteen.
They should treat you differently
and assign you to be an orderly
or a telegraph operator
or to do any kind of service
far away from the frontier."

For many years I couldn't promise you, Mom.
I was not sure whether I could endure
the wolfhounds the Russians would set upon me
if I refused to tell what they wanted to know.

The First Photograph

Although it was snowing that Sunday
we all gathered at the little photo-house,
which was the only one in Hunchun County,
to take our first photograph as a new soldier.
Two submachine guns were passed from hand to hand.
Everybody by turns stood before the camera
with the gun held before his breast.
When my turn came I was so nervous
that our squad-leader laughed and said:
"Don't let the gun break your neck."
Someone in the back whispered:
"The gun makes him smaller."

Every one of us wanted to have some words
printed on his picture, because
we were going to send it home.
Someone chose: "Defend the Country with My Life!"
Someone chose: "Be Ready to Wipe Out the Invaders!"
Someone chose: "A Brave Guard at the Northern Frontier!"
I chose: "Forever Hold Tight My Steel Gun!"

Marching towards Martyrdom

The commander gave orders
and we started marching.
We swung our hands vigorously up to our second buttons,
and watched each other through the corners of our eyes
to keep our bodies in a straight line.
We marched as if we were on parade,
although we knew these were exercises.

But we stopped before a deep trash pit,
and kept marching in place on its edge.

"Go ahead! Who told you to stop?
If you kill yourselves
your families will know you are martyrs!"

We marched on.

It was so easy to become a martyr,
and there were so many ways.

Active Defense

You, special-task company,
must be ready to stab into the enemy's side
like a sharp knife
which opens a stomach.

If a fight breaks out,
your task is to cross the border
and take that treeless hill.
You must do it at night.
So you will be a needle
stuck in the enemy's throat.
In military terms
this is called "active defense."

Remember there is no border-line in war,
and do whatever is necessary for us.
From now on, all your exercises
must be designed to fulfill this task.

I shuddered.
We came here
to defend the sacred
                    border-
                    line.

A Battalion-Commander Complains to His Secretary

This morning I again talked with Wang Yong's mother
for two hours. It was no use.
She still believes that I am the man who can
decide whether to nominate her son as a martyr or not.
Damn it, if I could issue the martyr card
I would give it to every one in our battalion,
dead or alive. She cried this morning
begging me for help and said she would not leave
without getting the martyrship for her son.

I well understand her situation.
With a son killed like that she and her family
can't raise their heads among their folk.
If I got killed that way my wife
or my mother would do the same thing.
But everybody knows Wang Yong did not go to
the military exercise that day
and he got his head knocked off
while fooling with a mortar in the barracks.
Our battalion is already notorious for the accident.

Well, she had her reasons and insisted
her son died at the frontier and for the country.
I did not deny that and told her
we could write a letter to the Military Department
in her county saying her son died for the country.
But she is a smart woman and knows she can get nothing
from the local Military Department. She sticks with us.
I even tried to buy her over. I asked:
"How is the financial situation of your family?"
She was so quick-witted that she snapped back,
"I don't want any money. I want the name for my son!"
She was right. That's a mother.

Now what can we do? I can't order her to leave.
It was in our hands that she lost her boy
but it is impossible to get the name for her son.
Maybe we'd better let her stay as long as she wants
and treat her well until she is tired of us.

A Forced March

In the white tranquil world
we walked 40 miles a day
with guns, baggage, food,
and even a 70-lb. transmitter.
We had only one horse
loaded with our field cauldrons.
Twelve girls went with us.
They carried medical boxes and telephones.
One night, after a whole day's journey,
we started a forced march.
We ran like a large pack of roe deer
hunted by leopards. On the road
were scattered our mittens, mugs and toothbrushes.
The girls were exhausted and could not move.
We dragged them like hauling
weeping sheep into a slaughter-house.
Only warm breaths came out of their mouths
with groaning words, "drop— me——
Let— me— die—"

We ran 5 miles in 53 minutes.

How can I congratulate you
on your sister's joining the army?

A Hero's Mother Blames
Her Daughter

Every time you come home you make me angry.
You accuse me of being vain, and loving
the name of the Hero's Mother. Today
I don't want to quarrel with you.
I just want to speak up so that
you may understand I'm not such a bad woman.

After your elder brother died in the fight
with the Russians on Zhenbao Island,
I did send your younger brother to the army
and let him fight the enemy like his brother.
It was not because I lost my senses
and wanted to enhance my honor as the Hero's Mother.
Is there any mother who would choose
to sacrifice her own son for such fame?
Listen! The country was in danger at that time
and your younger brother was already a big man.
With or without the example of your elder brother
he should go to the army. It is men's duty
to defend the country. I was not wrong in this.

After your younger brother got killed in an accident
while digging a tunnel with his comrades,

I sent you to the army. I tell you I was not
a heartless mother. You're a part of my flesh too;
besides, you were the only child I could keep.
Let Heaven witness, I did not mean to send you
to fight like a man, although I did say:
"Let her take over the gun left by her brothers."
This time I knew you would not get killed
because they would try every way to protect you.
But if I did not send you to the army,
how could you leave our poor remote village?
how could you become a doctor as you are now?
how could you marry a good handsome man?
how could you live in Beijing with your son
going to the best primary school?

I didn't hesitate when I sent your younger brother away.
But in your case it took me many days to decide.
One night I made up my mind and prayed
to your dead father and your elder brother:
"This is Rongrong's only chance.
I must not let her miss it.
Whatever happens to me I can endure.
Please protect her on her way."

Now your horns are strong and you turn around
to gore your mother. If I did anything wrong,
I did it for you. You are the person who benefits.
What did I get from it? Two martyr cards?
Do you think I can live on them?
Do you think I enjoy looking at them!

Anybody may have the right to blame me
except you. You don't have the right to do it!

My Knowledge of the Russian Language

It was stupid to tell you
that I knew a little Russian.
You were so pleased,
as if I was a jar of the best caviar
which you found
while holding a glass of vodka.
You grasped my hand and your eyes looked wild.
You poured out some Russian words
that sounded like a flock of swans
                    flying out of a lake.

I could not answer you in Russian.
You must have thought I was a fake,
for you released my hand,
lowered your eyes,
and let silence prove my guilt.

But I do know a little Russian.
The first sentence I learned was:
"Put Down Your Arms!"
The last sentence I could shout was:
"Hands Up! Follow Me!"

two   *The Dissolution
of a Kingdom*

My Kingdom

When we played house
you all assigned me to be the king
since there wasn't another boy among us.
But I was a small clumsy king
who did not know how to conduct myself imperially,
or how to rule my harem in our dormitory,
or how to treat the queen differently from the concubines,
or how to command all the amazons to defend our building,
or how to employ my maids
to look after my food and my bed.
Yet I was the king,
a small peacock in a large flock.

My kingdom was a little paper ship
launched into the Pacific Ocean.
It sank every minute,
but it went down slowly for many years,
and none of us was aware of its sinking.
It disintegrated step by step
losing you one after another
who swam away from my ship
and changed into the mermaids
serving the Dragon of Fate in the Water Palace

until finally my princess deserted her boyish father
until at the bottom of the dark sea
I was crawling as a lonely crab.

A Sacred Mango

We gathered in front of our City Hall
exploding firecrackers and beating drums and gongs.
Thousands of people came over
to receive a gift for our city from Chairman Mao.
It was a golden mango carried by a big truck
accompanied by three other trucks,
all of which were planted with colorful flags
and loaded with golden chrysanthemums.

The mango was exhibited in the center of a hall.
We lined up to look at it
and to show our gratitude and respect.

But that night
some curious child tasted the fruit
and was not caught.
Our mayor was frightened and outraged,
"Damn it, if I knew which son of a rabbit bit the mango
I would turn his whole family
into counter-revolutionaries!"

But what could we do?
We substituted a wooden mango for the real one.

A Page from a Schoolboy's Diary

Radio Beijing broadcast the victorious news
that seventy-four American airplanes had been shot down.
How happy we were sitting around a radio set
and how proud we are of our Vietnamese uncles
who shoot down the American airplanes
like killing sparrows with an air gun.

Our school has decided to hold a big celebration,
as people did in Beijing yesterday,
to support the heroic Vietnamese people
and to condemn the American ghouls.
There will be a call for donation
and I am sure all the teachers and students
will give whatever they have. I will present
my eighty-five cents pocket money to the Vietnamese.
It doesn't matter not to have candies for some months.

We already had a writing competition last week.
The topic was: "What Shall I Do
in Supporting Vietnam and Fighting the U.S.?"
I did not win the competition

because my pen was not strong.
Mingming got the first prize.
She ended her essay with such a powerful sentence:
"As a child I must cherish
the aspiration to drive the American wolves
away from the earth some day!"
We congratulated her and promised her
we would do the same thing when we grew up.

Because We Dare Not Be Ambitious

We were all tame children
with modest aspirations.
That morning
when our teacher called our names
we stood up and answered timidly:
when we grew up we wanted to be
a soldier, a teacher,
a worker, or a peasant.
But you unscrupulously declared:
"My ideal is to be
the President of our country."

Our teacher was scared out of her wits,
and we all burst into laughter.
Even you too laughed
like a little cock standing on a granary
greeting a big rising sun.

The following day you were assigned
to light the stove in our classroom

for the whole winter.
For many years we would call you
"President Wang,"
and gossip behind you,
"He is the greatest ass."

Our Words

Although you were the strongest boy in our neighborhood
you could beat none of us. Whenever
we fought with you we would shout:
"Your father was a landlord.
You are a bastard of a blackhearted landlord."
Or we would mimic your father's voice
when he was publicly denounced:
"My name is Li Wanbao. I was a landlord;
before liberation I exploited my hired hands
and the poor peasants. I am guilty
and my guilt deserves ten thousand deaths."
Then you would withdraw your hard fists
and flee home cursing and weeping like a wild cat.

You fought only with your hands,
but we fought with both our hands and our words.
We fought and fought and fought
until we overgrew you and overgrew ourselves,
until you and we were sent to the same village
working together in the fields

sharing tobacco and sorghum spirits at night
and cursing the brigade leader behind his back
when he said: "You, petty bourgeoisie,
must take your 're-education' seriously!"

Until none of us had words.

A production brigade was a subunit of a commune at that time.

A Thirteen-Year-Old Accuses His Teacher

How many times you talked to us
about the bravery of those revolutionary martyrs
who never gave up under the unbearable tortures!
They were tied on "tiger-benches"
with hot bricks on their feet.
They were forced to see their comrades shot
and remained unshakable. The enemies
even hammered long bamboo pikes into each of their fingers,
yet they couldn't break their will.
"My dear students," you said to us,
"imagine how painful it was.
Every finger is connected with the heart.
But our heroes never gave up!"

When the Red Guards came for you,
you were very tame. They slapped your face.
You were so scared that you couldn't speak.
During the denunciation you repeated whatever you were told.
You even called yourself "an egg of a turtle."
The following morning I saw you running in a team
of "Monsters and Demons." You shouted with them,

"Leniency to those who confess;
severity to those who refuse!
We are all counter-revolutionaries
deserving ten thousand deaths!
We must cast off our old self
and start a new life!"

How could you expect me to attend your class
again listening to you as your "dear student"?

Not Because We Did Not Want to Die

How often we talked about how to die?
You could use your soft scarf to hang yourself.
You could drink a bowl of DDT.
You could take a bottle of sleeping pills.
You could climb up a water tower
        and fly down without an umbrella
        but with your head towards the ground.
You could tie a stone to your back
        and jump into a reservoir.
· · · · ·

There were so many ways to die.
Any of them could be better than
to be "re-educated" in that village,
sowing, hoeing, getting in crops,
laying bricks, loading carts,
and even leveling up graves;
better than to be racing
for 18 hours with an endless day;
better than to only have
five days break for a whole year.

We thought none of us was
courageous and cruel enough to die,
leaving our parents
to cry their hearts and eyes out.
Every night, the five of us laughed and smoked,
teasing each other about
how to perform a painless death.
But sometimes we collapsed
and were soaked with tears.

Then one morning Xiaoling said she was sick
and did not go to the chicken farm.
When we returned at night she was sound asleep.
She slept for five days until her heart stopped.

After that, we smiled and were filled with gratitude.
She was much stronger than any of us,
and demonstrated for all of us
with her tiny little bones.

We, four young girls, survived.
We survived, not because we wanted to.

A Happy Night

After twenty years' hard labor in the pig farm
yesterday morning you were told
your reputation was rehabilitated
and you were invited back to the city
where you had worked as an editor.

Last night you smiled at us,
for the first time blissfully.
We chattered and drank wine with the sausages
which we had agreed to keep for a special day.
Even the cigarettes in our hands
were shining like stars in our little shed.
You talked about your future plan
and said you were just forty-eight
and still had many years to do many things.
You talked and talked
until your tongue was too thick for words.
Yet you laughed and laughed
as if you had won the Marathon.

This morning everybody got up early
to see you off, but you didn't rise.
We couldn't wake you up.
You slept carelessly on your brick bed.

The Execution of a Counter-Revolutionary

It is no use to beg anymore.
He has begged them many times
to let me speak to the head of the army hospital,
but he's told nobody will listen to him,
a bad-egg, who only deserves a bullet.

"We've been ordered to get your skin,"
the squad-leader says, "to repair
the extensive burns of Liu Yi
who risked his own life
saving horses from the burning stable.
Now, let's go."

They take him to the hill behind the hospital.

It's dinner time
and the loudspeaker is playing music.
Nobody will hear the shot in the woods.

They stop at a ruined temple
whose stones, bricks and rafters
have been ripped off by the villagers.

In the distance
a light is shining like a glow-worm.
He doesn't know whether it's a star or a lamp.
It doesn't matter now.
He takes it as the pole-star.
His only worry is: I'm not nineteen yet
and my parents will never know
how their son disappeared.

"Now you may say something if you want."
They pull out the towel from his mouth and wait.

Suddenly he starts yelling, "I curse all of you,
the whole hospital! All your babies
will have no ass-holes and die at birth!
I curse Liu Yi and his family too!
He and his folks will be struck by thunderbolts!"
They raise their pistols
and he raises his tied hands:
"Long live the Chinese Communist Party!
Long live—"
One pistol fires.

He wanted to shout "Chairman Mao,"
but they wouldn't let him get it out.

The bullet hit his penis—
which is the best way to save the skin.

Gift

Don't be angry at me, father.
How could I forget my root!

Even if one has money
it is not easy to choose a proper gift.
Even if one has chosen a proper gift
it is difficult to find the right person
who will accept your gift and also help you
and who will not just "swallow" your gift
telling you how hard he has tried,
yet it didn't work out.

But this was not our case.
We already located the right person
who worked in the Personnel Department.
Our neighbor told us the guy would "savor" gifts.
We decided to present him a watch,
a good little piece for his daughter's wedding.
But we did not have the money.

For a whole afternoon you walked
from one shop to another to see

where the price of the watch was the lowest.
You journeyed around the city
with broken sandals on your feet
and with only a few coins in your pocket.

Having succeeded in borrowing the money
from Liu Yi I immediately started
searching for you in the streets.
When I found you, it was too late.
The shop where the price was the lowest
was closed. On our way home
you scolded me for being unable to
take care of myself as a man of twenty.
You kept saying: "Remember
this day, Shaoming, my son.
Remember how your father
dragged around his old bones
helping you to get the job!"

I remember everything, father.
But if I had not accepted
Old Wang's lamp just now
he would believe I refused to help him.
Tonight he would knock around to look for
another gift or another person.
Many people would "savor" his gift
but few can help him get the residence card.

It is impossible to be a clean official.

I'll give him something back
at the Spring Festival.

A Brother's Advice

Don't be chicken, my brother.
Tell the manager and the party secretary in your factory
that they will not have a good time
if they don't give you a raise.
Don't let them think
our Liang family is full of soft eggs.
Sometimes it's no use to beg.
Let me tell you how I did it last fall.

When my company was assigning new apartments
I was told that my name was not on the list.
I begged around and spent a lot of money on gifts.
Still I couldn't get my name on the list.
They ignored me as if I was a fly
which only buzzes but doesn't bite.
Then I began telling everybody that
if they don't give me an apartment I would
stab both the party secretary and the manager.
Fuck his grandmother, this time it worked.
Two weeks later they assigned me a brand-new apartment.
Some of my fellow-workers, who were not

on the list originally, got new apartments too.
I guess the leaders did not want our fellow workers
to see that they were scared by me,
so they assigned apartments to
some other fellows at the same time.

My brother, don't begin by begging them.
Even the devil is afraid of an evil person.
If you can't be an evil guy, at least
pretend to be one this time.

three

No Tears for Love

The Haircut

When we quarreled last time
you promised to give me a special haircut.
Yesterday you fulfilled your word
by shaving my head bald.

You could not straighten your body
and laughed until tears came to your eyes.
How proud you were
while telling your friends
about the masterwork at home!
Our daughter laughed too.
She laughed,
for her daddy's head was shining like a bulb.

In fact, I also laughed at myself,
for when I lost my first love
I shaved my head the same way.
In our town everybody sighed and shook his head
seeing me walking in the streets
without my dark curly hair
except the girl I loved
who laughed and loved my haircut.

A Young Worker's Lament to His Former Girlfriend

Because I couldn't love our late Premier more than I love you
you accused me of being a man without heart.
There was no use to explain and you
simply swept me away as if I were a weasel.
I never had the fortune, as you did,
of being chosen from eight hundred students in a school
to tie a red scarf around his neck;
besides, he never visited the small town where I grew up.
I saw him in movies and read about him in newspapers.
I agree he was a good man working for the people day and night.
When he passed away, I also cried like any of you,
but still I couldn't love him more than I love you.

I know how the dimples bloom when you smile.
I know how the eyes dim when you're shy.
I know how the waist wavers when you walk.
I know how the nose turns up when you scold.
How could you want me to love him more than I love you?

If only you and I were twenty years younger
or eighty years older, so that
we could love without him!

An Editor Meets His Former Girlfriend in a Fish House

If I could tell you a lie it would do.
It was the truth that destroyed.
If I had an oily tongue
or you had distorting ears
it might also do. What bad luck,
I was doomed to say it
and you were doomed to hear
that you could never be Mrs. Thatcher,
a strong woman, as you dreamed to be,
with great power and also a happy family.

Today I am lining up to buy some fish
and you are lining up too
with your baby in your arms
to buy your portion of hairtail.
It is not easy to have a good Spring Festival.
"Why don't you find a place to rest yourself, Ling?
I can stand in the line for you.
When it's your turn I'll let you know.
Give me your basket."

How sound the baby is asleep!

It could be mine.
If only I could tell *you* a lie.

An Old Novelist's Will

I won't leave you there alone
in the ash-room on the hill,
sharing the cold shelves with other homeless souls.
Now at last you have come home
and stay at the top of the chest in my room.
There is no picture on your box.
I told them to take it off
for I don't want to see your old face.

It is not a miracle but an accident
that you survived all the sixty years
believing me still alive
who had always thought you were dead.
You were such a stubborn girl that
at your last moment you were murmuring my name
and waiting for me to come to your side,
although I was an old crow, hundreds of miles away,
which could not fly.

I do not hate your family any more
who did not allow you to marry me

because we had the same family name.
If love persists hate dissolves.
Nor do I blame you for refusing
to elope with me, who was then a poor teacher
and couldn't even fill my own stomach.
Nor do I regret having declined to see you
in recent years after I came to know
you were still alive. I was afraid
you might be disappointed with my crumpled face
which was no longer a map of love and mystery.
I did not want to see *your* sorrowful face either.
Let us remain the young lovers in my book,
An Oasis Under the Moon, which I dedicated to you.

Now we are together and I am satisfied.
I know you are still hungry, but please wait.
I have told my daughter that after I am dead
she must put half my ashes
in your box and the other half with her mother.
I said to her, "If I commit bigamy,
let the King of Hell punish me."
She has promised. Please be patient,
my dear. Be a good girl.

Our Date on the Bridge

Although I am a handsome girl
and well-known in our province
as the leader of "The Iron Girl Team,"
I will not be anyone's wife.
The pains and toil I have been suffering
must not be passed down to my children
who shall not come into this world.

The labor of the go-between is useless
though I did come to this bridge to meet you
so as not to disappoint my parents.
You welcomed me without a greeting.
I know you know my mind.
Let us stand together and be silent
watching the cold deep water
flowing beneath our feet.

Our dumb show has lasted for half an hour.
If you jump into the river

I will join you there.

S n o w

You sent me the news of snow
which is handsome and cold.

Snowflakes are falling through my fingers.
They are covering stars
and the foot-prints on the mountain slope.

Below the mountain
pines quietly bend their green branches.

For you, I am standing
on the empty mountain top,
for a long, long time.

You sent me the feeling of snow
and want me to be both your man
and your snowman.

four   *Ways*

Ways

Two ways lie under my feet with different promises.
One leads to an orchard full of pears and apricots,
and the other to a gallery which has a movie-room.

Since my mind cannot make a choice between the two,
each of my legs follows its own will.
I see my right foot walking vigorously on the right way
and my left foot marching confidently on the left one.

By having taken both ways
I have turned my head into a red balloon
which pursues an upward way.

Begging

It is so rich
to know in this world
someone is begging for you.

This afternoon
I find an old man
begging around in this city
for *me*.
He walks into one lane and another
without a bowl in his hand.
He begs from door to door
with his grey beard and ancient words.
He is not a beggar,
but today he begs specially for me.
He does it secretly.

Following him without his notice
I come to know
I must not be
afraid of dogs
or ashamed of myself.

To an Ancient Chinese Poet

That night you were very drunk.
You banged your pipa on a stone table.
The moon could not set up
the upset cups scattered around,
although it was sharpening your saber
standing on a single-log bridge.
The poems on scraps of paper were gone with the breeze.
You allowed them to fall into a river
which abounded with tadpoles and apple blossoms.

"What's the use of fame as a poet?"
you yelled at the foggy night,
"It's a silent affair a thousand years after me.
After me!" You raised your empty hand,
"Let me drink," and fell to the ground,
"Let me sleep." You were
fast asleep on the precipice.

It is a thousand years now.
Today, I put my hand into another river

whose water is clear and warm.
Tadpoles and apple blossoms
are flowing through my fingers
while the cold passion of your poems
is penetrating through my arm.

*A plucked string instrument with a fretted fingerboard, the
pipa is the traditional instrument played by ancient Chinese
poets.*

To My Aunt

When I was a small boy,
how often you told me
after you had quarreled with your old man:
"If I had the money
to buy two packages of pastry
I would eat all of them
and die happily."
For many years I wondered
why you did not have such little money
and what would happen
if you had the money in your hand.
You might jump into the well behind your yard,
or lay yourself on the railroad track at night,
or hold a bare electric wire
with tears in your eyes and pastry in your mouth,

.   .   .   .   .   .

Your old man has retired now.
He fishes and hunts every day
and sometimes hums some clumsy tunes.
You have money now, but there are

too many kinds of pastry to choose.
You have your own little grocery store
and two lovely grandsons. You are
too rich to be able to afford any death.

A Young Woman Scientist
Writes to Her
Three-Year-Old Son

Thank you for the pictures you drew for us.
What a pity, your daddy did not see them
before he left with the army for the frontier.
He would adore them
and show them to his comrades-in-arms.
The dog looks like a real dog
and the elephant is the one
we saw together in the Victory Zoo last summer.

In the letter your grandpa said,
"Nan-Nan is a good boy and likes to be clean.
Whenever his clothes are soiled
he wants to change them.
But still he doesn't want to
have a haircut or to get his head washed."
You are such a clean boy.
I don't understand why
you are so careless about your head.
If you don't wash your head, by and by
some worms will live in your hair.
If you don't have your hair cut often,

you will become a little hotchpotch.
You are a sensible child and know
how to take care of your own head
and not to burden grandpa.

Your daddy misses you all the time.
Now he is at the frontier to defend
our country and protect our home.
He will be all right.
He promised me he would be back.
Before he left, whenever he came in at night,
he would look at your photos and speak to you.
Sometimes he asked me in your little voice,
"What's this Mummy? What's that Mummy?
Why is a watermelon round, Mummy?"
Then we both laughed
and talked about you, our good boy.
O, if only we three could be together,
even if just one hour a week.

Right now I am studying germs.
Not those ugly bad germs that kill people
but those good germs friendly to people.
You may be surprised that there are good germs.
In fact, not all germs are man's enemies.
We need some germs to make bread, wine,
and many other things.
Even the sweets you eat
can't be made without germs.

After I finish the work I will
have two weeks vacation for this year.
I will come home and play with you.
But I have to wait for your daddy

so that we three can spend some time together.
We will bring you a lot of good things.
Whatever you want please tell us,
or just draw some pictures of them.

Let me kiss your little apple face, Nan-Nan.
May you make more progress.

An Older Scholar's Advice

After you get your master's degree
you will have to work hard for some years
to be promoted to a lectureship. Then you can relax.
Don't think that if you go on working in that way
you can get your professorship. First,
you must have enough teaching experience.
In my school, only after having taught for 24 years
will you be qualified for consideration
as an associate professor. Second,
you must publish enough papers.
It is not hard to write them but it is not easy
to publish them. In fact, you can publish anything
if you have connections; my colleagues told me that
publication is also an important field of study.
Well, if you "study" it thoroughly
you may be able to get your papers out,
but you will have to pay a lot for it.

For me the most practical thing to do now
is not to worry about my professorship.
So many lecturers are not qualified for it
until they are qualified for retirement

or for death. I just ignore it for the time being.
In the morning I practice Tai Chi.
In the evening I watch TV and go to bed early.
I have quit smoking but drink two cups of wine
every day. Wine can warm your blood.
Don't indulge yourself in sex.
It will weaken your young kidneys.
As long as you are in good health,
as long as you live longer than others,
eventually you will get your professorship.

You can wait for that.

A Rumor

A rumor is launched into the sky.
It is exploding in the air
turning a dull night splendid.

The rumbling cracks,
the dazzling colors,
the ever-changing shapes,
and even the smell of the smoke
excite the people
who just finished dinner
and don't know how to kill the night.
All of them gossip, smile,
and exchange opinions about the show,

except one person
who, from now on,
groans every night.

A General's Comments on a Politician

He is no politician
because he has rubber hands
and doesn't know it is necessary to kill.
He watched his enemies developing in eggs,
and observed how they broke the eggs
and became nestlings.
He thought they were chickens,
but one day they flew to the sky
and changed into hawks.
He doesn't have the guts to crush the eggs!

When I was a battalion commander,
our neighbor battalions always suffered
from the enemy's artillery.
They knew there were some agents in their units
who informed the enemy of their movements,
but they couldn't find them out.
This never happened to my battalion,
because I did not bother to find them out.
I just shot the few persons I suspected.
As the head of a whole battalion

I could not put four hundred lives at stake.
To be sure, I did it secretly. At night
I brought them to a grove one by one.

A politician must have iron hands,
although you may wear gloves over them;
just as a general must never worry about
how many wronged ghosts cry
after he puts his sword into its sheath.

An Old Red Guard's Reply

Having been wrecked so many times
we will not set sail once more.
Having been deceived again and again
nobody could care whether there is any truth.
Try to persuade us,
portraying the magnificent deeds of the old days
or promising us a golden monument in the archives.

Our old hearts, burnt out by dreams, fell
like meteors on the shore
and transformed into these rocks
that cannot be shaken by the great waves.
Our legs were amputated on the tables
which we once mistook as stages
where we enacted the Dance of Loyalty.

Now we cannot move,
either toward the sea or toward the land.
Whatever you say, our tongues,
which finally have learned how to voyage,
will reply, "Yes sir."

A Photograph from China

At our last dinner you told me
you had delayed so long to go back
because you could not shut your mouth.

The photograph you sent me
shows how happy you are back
with your wife and kids.
Behind you the winding paths
look the same on the Small-Monk Mountain.
It is so tranquil.

Still, I am worried
about your smiling mouth.

Because I Will Be Silenced

Once I have the freedom to say
my tongue will lose its power.
Since my poems strive to break the walls
that cut off people's voices,
they become drills and hammers.

But I will be silenced.
The starred tie around my neck
at any moment can tighten into a cobra.

How can I speak about coffee and flowers?